THE LIBRARY OF INTERIOR DETAIL

CASA

THE LIBRARY OF INTERIOR DETAIL

CASA

Southern
Spanish Style

ELIZABETH HILLIARD

PHOTOGRAPHS BY JOHN MILLER

BULFINCH PRESS
LITTLE, BROWN AND COMPANY
BOSTON • NEW YORK • TORONTO • LONDON

First North American Edition

ISBN 0-8212-2174-4

Library of Congress Catalog Card Number 94-73027

Bulfinch Press is an imprint and trademark of
Little, Brown and Company (Inc.)
Published simultaneously in Canada by
Little, Brown and Company (Canada) Limited

PRINTED IN SINGAPORE

A flimsy cupboard door, with cut-out star or flower shapes for decoration, has been transformed into the door of a room by having a strip of wood added to its top and bottom. This door was bought from the famous gypsies of Ronda, who organize architectural reclamation as well as making new traditional furniture from pine.

INTRODUCTION

THE STYLE OF SOUTHERN SPAIN IS AS DISTINCTIVE AS THE MAGNIFICENT FESTIVAL regalia of a matador – no-one could possibly mistake it for anything else. And, like the matador's costume, it has its origins in traditions formed in centuries past. If the north of Spain, and the city of Barcelona in particular, is perceived as being the powerhouse of all things modern in art, design, architecture and interiors, so the south, and Andalucia in particular, is keeper of a large part of Spain's decorative past.

Just the word 'Andalucia' conjures up poetic images which speak of the Moors, southern Spain's Arab inhabitants for hundreds of years. The influence of their philosophy concerning buildings and gardens is felt even today. The play of brilliant sunlight on the slender columns of pavilions in the exquisite Alhambra Palace in Granada, striped horseshoe arches in the mosque of Cordoba, geometric patterns on panels of gleaming coloured tiles, inner paved courtyards, palm trees, still pools of water and above all, the sound of fountains playing: these are among the elements which, together, give southern Spanish style its historical resonance.

The influence of the Moors is ingrained in the imagination of Andalucians, as Gerald Brennan, an Englishman who went to live in a remote part of Andalucia immediately after the First World War, soon discovered. In his charming book *South of*

Granada, which describes his years in Yegen, he wrote, 'When I first arrived in the village and spoke of the war in which I had been taking part, many people supposed I had been fighting the Moors.'

Southern Spain's early history is colourful and dramatic. Successive invasions by Phoenicians, Greeks, Celts and Carthaginians gave way in the first century BC to settlement by the Romans, who founded the city of Cordoba, later famous for its mosque and the flowering of Islamic scholarship. Phoenicians are supposed to have given Spain her name, from their word for rabbit, 'sapan'(at the time Spain was heavily wooded and was overrun with rabbits). Visigoths subsequently conquered the Iberian peninsula in the fifth century.

Each race of settlers brought with them creative skills and styles, some of which became absorbed into the indigenous culture. The Celts and Visigoths, for example, were superb ironsmiths who made the most of Spain's great metal deposits. They introduced skills developed to ever greater heights by fifteenth- and sixteenth-century artists and artisans and still venerated in modern times by people of taste. Metal deposits are still mined at the site of ancient excavations in western Andalucia, making them the oldest mines in the world.

The two types of metalwork you are most likely to see in Spain today are the locks, studs and decorative straps on old wooden chests and doors, and *rejas*. The latter are the heavy and often elaborately wrought old iron grilles covering the street-facing windows of houses in cities, towns and villages. These served the purpose not only of keeping out brigands and other intruders but also of protecting your unmarried daughters within. As late as the early twentieth century, a well-brought-up young woman in Seville or Granada only ever saw her *novio*, or boyfriend, through this grille (or from an upstairs balcony) until they were formally betrothed.

Dappled sunlight falls on the reja *of an old door in a village near Seville.*

The great period of Moorish culture in Andalucia lasted from early in the eighth century, when the Moors invaded and conquered the Visigoth kingdom, until January 1492, when the 'Catholic Monarchs', Isabella and Ferdinand, recaptured Granada. The Moors inevitably brought a great influx of Islamic culture, developed in the near east and incorporating influences which included the Byzantine and Roman. This met and absorbed many deep-rooted indigenous skills and styles, to emerge with a strong, energetic, confident, individual and almost fully formed identity of its own. Above all, though it had much in common with Islamic styles in other countries, it was distinctively Iberian.

The Spanishness that characterizes every period of Spain's artistic heritage is due in part to the geography of the Iberian peninsula, which is almost a huge island, joined to the rest of Europe by a stretch of unfriendly Pyrenean mountains three hundred miles (roughly five hundred kilometres) wide. In the south, it stretches to within nine miles (about fifteen kilometres) of Africa. The only neighbouring country with which it shares the peninsula is Portugal, a fraction of its size.

One example of the sort of marriage behind what we think of as Moorish style is the traditional layout of a Moorish home, which in fact combined Christian, Roman and Islamic ideas in a model of perfection. In Islam, the sky framed by the perimeter of your courtyard is your own little piece of heaven. The principles of garden design which the Moors introduced were based on rhythm and geometry, encapsulated in an enclosed garden or courtyard with pillared porticoes and pavilions. Paradise is portrayed as a garden in Islam, as it is in other religions, including Christianity with its Garden of Eden. Meanwhile the plan of the house, with rooms opening onto the central courtyard, is inherited from the Romans.

The importance of having a palm tree in your courtyard (as opposed to any other tree) goes back to a Moorish caliph, founder of the great mosque of Cordoba and of the Umaiyad dynasty of rulers. He is said to have planted one of the first date palms in Spain to remind himself of Syria, his homeland. Among other things he was a poet, and described himself as an 'immigrant stranger', akin to his lonely palm. Later in the same caliphate, which lasted for three centuries, there are believed to have been over fifty thousand verdant gardens in Cordoba, varying in size but most of them organized around the all-important palm tree.

The Koran describes paradise as 'a garden flowing with streams'. When Granada became the capital of the Moorish territories, the Darro river was diverted, by means of a feat of engineering, from the valley below to the top of the mountain, where the Alhambra Palace now stands. Water makes a vital and magical contribution to the Alhambra's spellbinding atmosphere. In the Court of Myrtles it is perfectly still, lying in a long and narrow rectangular pool which reflects the shrubs and buildings alongside; in the Court of Lions it is constantly moving, shimmering in the basin and burbling in the fountain and the jets that fall from the lions' mouths.

In architecture, the Moorish detail which is most often to be found in Andalucian homes today is the horseshoe arch. This juts out slightly where the arch meets the vertical sides of the archway opening. The most spectacular example of the use of arches in Andalucian architecture is the mosque at Cordoba. Here, hundreds of pillars support striped arches, with yet more arches rising up above the first tier. The effect is enthralling, the geometry and repetition of lines and arcs managing to be restful and thrilling at the same time. The well-known travel writer H.V. Morton visited Spain in the 1950s and described his impression of the mosque in *A Stranger in Spain*:

The entrance to the renovated olive press attached to an old senorial house and chapel near Seville. Oil is made in presses in the village once again.

In the morning I went to the mosque of Cordoba, with no intention of allowing myself to be carried away by enthusiasm, but in two minutes I was vanquished. Of all the buildings of the Islamic world this is to me the most fantastic … It reminds me of an immense forest full of zebras. The striped red and white arches stretch away in innumerable vistas, and whichever way you look you see the same view. It is like a trick with mirrors, yet the feeling it roused in me was one of delight … What ought to have been a failure was a brilliant success.

The furnishing of southern Spanish houses can appear sparse. There is no great amount of old or antique furniture available to anyone decorating a home. Spain does not have the same tradition of fine furniture as is found in some other parts of Europe. Even in grand houses pieces tend to be robust and often heavily carved. In the whole country, there have been few great designers and craftsmen whose names stand out in the history of furniture, as do Chippendale and Sheraton in England, for example. Added to which, quantities of old furniture are thought to have been burnt as fuel during the desperate years of the Civil War.

Those pieces which do exist in Andalucia are fairly rough and ready. They mostly consist of folding chairs and folding x-shaped stools, their forms derived from Visigoth and Moorish pieces which folded to make them easily transportable. Other items which can be found are traditional chests and occasional *bargueños* (table-top writing desks), or simple peasant furniture.

Some modern pine tables and chairs are made in the style of traditional peasant originals, the latter usually having rush seating. The Muños family, based in Ronda, is famous in contemporary Andalucia for making a thriving business out of manufacturing such furniture. A large family of gypsies with connections across the entire country, the Muñoses also have a firm grip on the architectural reclamation business. They can take the credit for having made a worthwhile industry out of saving great numbers of doors, *rejas* and other architectural antiques, in a country where enthusiasm for old buildings is confined to an enlightened élite.

One of the most extraordinary and distinctive pieces of furniture found in Andalucia is a type of round table called a *mesa camilla*. This has two tiers: the upper one at normal height serves as a table at which you sit; the lower one has a metal bucket set in the middle, in which burning charcoal is placed for heating. Houses in southern Spain do not have heating systems, the only heat coming from fireplaces and cookers. The *mesa camilla* offers a cosy place to sit on cool evenings and in winter. Gerald Brennan describes its use in *South from Granada*:

> This classic piece of furniture and the domestic rites accompanying it demand some explanation. Imagine then a circular deal table with a brazier of wood ash or charcoal set under it. Drape over it a red-flannel tablecloth that reaches on every side to the ground, and let three, four or six persons sit around it with the skirts of this tablecloth, which are split into sections, tucked about them. Let them have short coats or shawls thrown lightly over their backs and let their faces be leaning towards one another – either deep in a game of cards, or sewing, or else perfectly still and motionless, merely rippling the silence from time to time by some placid observation. Then you will have a picture of what family life is like during one half of the year in every town and village of this country.

Colours in Andalucian homes are often rich and strong, offset by brilliant white walls and blinding sunlight, or they are beautifully faded, mellow versions of their former selves, bleached by the sun. Reds, oranges, ochres, greens … the tones reflect the colours of the landscape, plants and flowers of the region. In the rest of Spain blue is not generally a popular colour because it is perceived as cool, even chilly, and because the dye was once rare and too costly to use. In Andalucia, however, the heat and brilliant sun counteract its coolness and blue is used to great effect.

Brilliant sunlight falling on a charmingly elaborate bell at the front gate of a house in Andalucia casts an intriguing pattern on the whitewashed wall behind.

Terracotta floors are used extensively and give warmth of colour to any room. They vary in tone depending on their age and, if they are new, on the method used to seal them. After being laid with a cement mortar, the tiles or thin bricks are cleaned with an astringent agent such as industrial vinegar. Then they are sealed, either with a modern silicone-based sealant, which does not darken the floor greatly, or with the more traditional linseed oil, which darkens and enriches the colour. Other possible sealants include paraffin and even petrol.

A pair of small wooden stools with inlaid seats, standing on a terracotta tiled floor,
(detail of the interior on page 51).

Typical Andalucian style, however, gives little space to textiles. Windows are small and generally have shutters rather than curtains. And furniture is usually wooden, though upholstered furniture and loose covers which would not look out of place in an English drawing room can be found in the homes of both foreigners and the more eclectic Spaniards. Another reason for the lack of fabrics is the climate. The strong sunlight and humidity is unkind to cloth, shortening its life considerably. Such textiles as there are tend to be cotton, linen and, occasionally, wool. Linen flax was traditionally grown in Galicia, but Franco's policies in the 1960s brought this to an end and today it is imported.

Much of the colour in a southern Spanish interior comes from ceramics – pottery and tiles. There is a long and rich history of ceramics in Spain. The Arabs are believed to have introduced refined oriental techniques, establishing potteries near Granada and Malaga. Here both tiles and ceramic vessels were made with metal lustre decoration – a technique which later went out of fashion and was lost, to be rediscovered in northern Europe in the nineteenth century.

Tiles are cool, practical and their glazed surfaces reflect light. Moorish architecture made extensive use of tiles for decoration, indoors and out, on every imaginable surface. Patterns included angular Cufic, and later flowing Cursive script for quotations from the Koran. Other semi-abstract decoration used plant forms, flowers, arabesques and geometric stars in patterns of such intricacy and variety that they created a feast for the eye.

Modern Spanish pottery varies greatly in design quality, the most attractive usually being the least pretentious. Simple, bold shapes and colourful, flowing decoration is the most pleasing and is found on jugs and mugs, plates, bowls and dishes of every shape and size. Decoration on the best modern tiles has a similarly unrestrained look and frequently uses star shapes and other motifs derived from Moorish designs. Another traditional type of ceramic which inspires modern tile makers is majolica ware, in which colourful pictures were painted onto tiles with green, blue and ochre-yellow glazes. This technique was introduced into Seville from Italy around 1500 by Francisco Niculoso. Original tiles from Moorish times and the Renaissance are very rare but not unheard-of in contemporary homes.

One person who was lucky enough to come across a cache of antique tiles is antique dealer Malcolm Davidson, who lives near Cadiz. Found in a barn, the tiles were laid out on the floor to be matched up before the major part was sold; fortunately there were sufficient left-over individual and small sets of tiles for the Davidsons and a neighbour to use in the construction of fireplaces. The tiles are believed originally to have decorated a palace in Seville or Cordoba, where they would have been used between the wooden beams to line a ceiling.

One of the great paradoxes of southern Spanish style is the huge gulf between the richness of Andalucian cultural heritage and common contemporary attitudes to anything antique. It is as great as the gulf in time between the Moors and modern Spain. Among most ordinary Spaniards (not including aristocrats, families with old money, the best designers and some artists and other people of taste) attitudes towards old buildings and their renovation, and indeed old things in general, vary little. They would rather have everything new: new clothes, new furniture, new houses.

A naturalized Spaniard, formerly an interior designer in England, points out:

> Spain is twenty years behind in many things, because of the years of repression caused by the Civil War in the 1930s and then the dictatorship of General Franco. Spaniards are catching up, but they still love everything new and plastic and they chuck out old things. I have found magnificent doors on skips. The movement to renovate old buildings is very new amongst ordinary people.

A detail of the fireplace on page 52 (left), showing close up the colour and delightfully lively decoration of the antique tiles with which it is inlaid.

Wicker baskets, old glass flagons and jars of local olives on a shelf above the cooker in the kitchen of an old house in Andalucia.

Added to this, the climate in Andalucia can be brutal. Sometimes after five summer months without rain you can hardly move or breath outdoors – and buildings, often badly built in the first place, suffer in the extremes. Eventually they rot or crumble and are pulled down. This lack of tenderness in the climate and in so many aspects of Andalucia applies to the treatment of old buildings. Much of the landscape and vegetation, the character of the people, even Flamenco singing and dancing, is harsh and uncompromising. Sacheverell Sitwell referred to this aspect of the country in 1961 when he wrote, 'No land in Europe, probably no other land in the civilized world, has so violent a personality, so strong a flavour, as that of Spain.'

Happily, those who do appreciate them find that the skills needed to restore, convert and extend their homes still exist among tradesmen and artisans. Building materials such as terracotta roof and floor tiles are still made in Andalucia, old windows and doors can be bought from the gypsies of Ronda as can new furniture based on old designs. Tiles and ceramics are plentiful. Using all these elements, the most splendid southern Spanish interiors bring together the old and the new, embracing Andalucia's magnificent heritage with contemporary vigour.

HALLS
& STAIRS

HALLWAYS OF ANDALUCIAN HOUSES DRAW YOU FROM THE OUTDOOR HEAT AND DUST, THROUGH A HEAVILY DEFENSIVE WOODEN DOOR BRAZENED WITH IRON STUDS AND STRAPS, INTO A COOL, TILED INTERIOR. TILED AND PAINTED STAIRWAYS LEAD YOU FURTHER AWAY FROM THE SUN. PLANTS AND TREES FLOURISH HERE, SHELTERED FROM THE BLISTERING BRIGHTNESS.

This front door of a casita is probably a hundred years old. The door-within-a-door is designed to let in a little light and obviate the need for a window. The tiled floor can be glimpsed within - square terracotta tiles with small glazed, coloured inserts.

*Massive old chestnut doors, original to this Andalucian house, open into the hall.
The lefthand door has a small hatch which opens to let in light and air when the doors are
closed against the sun's heat. Called a* postigo, *this one has its original lock. Locally-
made terracotta tiles cover the floor.*

The hall-cum-living room of artist Maria Foixa's home, with stairs leading to the next half-floor. The house, converted from storehouses belonging to the Archbishop of Seville, has a number of different levels. The walls of this room have been painted with ochre pigments and the stairs are lined below with antique tiles.

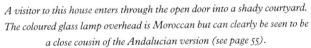

A visitor to this house enters through the open door into a shady courtyard. The coloured glass lamp overhead is Moroccan but can clearly be seen to be a close cousin of the Andalucian version (see page 55).

*A solid modern staircase with painted plaster sides and brightly painted risers
leads to bedrooms and a living room. Space underneath the stairs has been cleverly used to
provide storage for firewood.*

An elegant modern staircase built of bricks, plastered and painted ochre.
The treads have been laid with tiles and the stark, sinuous contours of the staircase are
softened with a mass of plants.

27

Detail of an old and pretty wrought-iron reja, *or window grille, retained for security on a window facing the street. Modern* rejas *do not have the same elegance and charm, being made in general from sheet metal.*

An exquisite mid-nineteenth-century wrought-iron gateway rescued from a demolished palace by reclamation dealers. The owner of this house fell in love with it, bought it, and then had to build a wall to accommodate it.

DOORS &
WINDOWS

Doors and windows in the houses of
southern Spain have a special charm.
Whether they are bold and massive
or small and delicate, they are always
interesting. Sometimes there is a door
within a door, or a window within a
window, or they are enlivened by carving
or a pretty *REJA* (window grille).

*A typical window within a door, the small hatch
allowing a little light and air to enter when the massive
studded front door is closed against intruders and
the searing heat.*

A small corner cupboard, installed when the house was converted from farm outbuildings about twenty years ago. Lattice work is frequently used for Andalucian cupboard doors, to allow some air to circulate in the hot climate. The pretty pottery lamp is Portuguese.

The front door of a house near Seville, parts of which are five hundred years old. The chandelier is modern, made locally and available in the Reina Carlotta shop in the village of Cazalla de la sierra near Seville, and by mail order (see Acknowledgements on page 80).

A hall cupboard painted white and aubergine. The hinges are a typical Andalucian design.

*A beautiful pair of carved wooden doors in Maria Foixa's sitting room
(see also pages 52 and 60).*

A splendid green-painted front door with iron studs and a decorative circular air vent. You turn a small handle inside to open and close the vent, according to the weather.

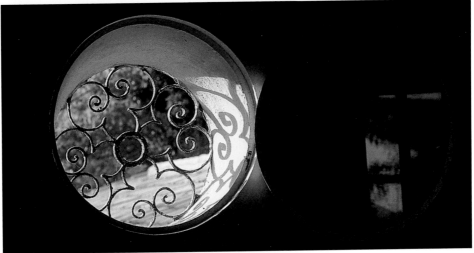

A very old wooden window (top) has recently had a smaller window made within one pane. This allows the owner to air the room without opening the whole window. The sill is covered with modern Spanish tiles. A small round window (above), with a charming wrought-iron reja, *brings extra ventilation into an upstairs bedroom.*

FLOORS, WALLS & CEILINGS

In southern Spanish houses, the natural materials from which floors, walls and ceilings are made can be seen in all their glory. Magnificent wooden beams support roofs and upper storeys; bare stone or terracotta and ceramic tiles and bricks cover floors; plaster walls are roughly painted.

A bunch of old keys giving access to the local church, hanging on a wall which has been rough-plastered and painted rusty red.

*Terracotta tiles from the Spain–Gibraltar border town of Lalinea, laid slightly off-line with
small, glazed, coloured inserts set in the gaps thus created. The sealant used here,
linseed oil, gives the floor a deeper tone than the finish on the tiles on page 45*

Left. *A very old door formed from miscellaneous planks of wood nailed together and painted white and grey. The floor is covered with blue and white marble tiles laid in a chequerboard pattern.*

Above. *A stone floor, original to the house, has been treated with linseed oil and varnish.*

Bougainvillea sprawls elegantly across an outside wall above a terracotta wall light of typical Andalucian design based on Arab originals.

A terracotta external wall-light of a design which has been in use for centuries, painted white like the wall behind it.

Riding hats hang on a rough-plastered and limewashed wall. The chair is an antique from Seville and the floor is covered with local tiles. In the background a horseshoe archway, its sides jutting slightly where they meet the arch itself, is painted a vibrant Andalucian blue.

These thin bricks, introduced by the Romans and still made today, were recently laid in a herringbone pattern, washed with vinegar and finished with a modern acrylic sealant to retain their pale colour. The chair is a Spanish antique and the shawl a mantón *of the type worn for processions and religious festivals.*

A magnificent and typically Andalucian ceiling built recently by the house's owner. The chestnut beams were made from trees growing on the adjoining farm which are thinned every four years.

Whitewashed walls support a wooden-beamed roof which has been lined with matting made from caña, *split cane, for greater warmth.* Caña *is found all over Spain and the matting is used not as a floor covering (it is too hard underfoot) but for blinds, roofing on terraces and, as here, as a ceiling liner.*

LIVING
SPACES

Living spaces are simply furnished, almost spartan. Their warmth comes from light reflected off walls painted rich, mellow colours or whitewashed. Blue is rarely used because it seems chilly, but when it does appear it creates a welcoming coolness in this searingly hot climate.

An exceptionally pretty, modern wrought-iron hanger for kitchen implements, based on an old design and now hung in a living room for decoration.

This seating area was created when agricultural buildings were converted into an elegant home in the late 1980s. The tiles were found in Seville, the pillars which form the legs of the table in Cortes, and the magnificent pot, once used for storing olive oil, in Lorca.

A cool, simple interior with a small sofa covered with a white linen loose cover. The floor is laid with large terracotta tiles. The effect is restrained and ascetic, the only touch of exoticism coming from the painting of a reclining woman.

An old granary, now converted and used as a meeting place for people involved in the arts in Andalucia. Rush seating is a typical feature of Spanish furniture. Pictures on the walls are collages made by the owner's mother from antique Peruvian textiles.

Maria Foixa's private sitting room. Walls are painted with glowing red pigments, the pair of painted doors is antique and an animal skin rug warms the tiled floor.

This magnificent fireplace is late nineteenth century and original to the house. On the left, the original cooking stove can just be seen. Here, a cocido, *bean and lentil stew, would have simmered all day awaiting the return of hungry farm workers. The rocking chair is typically Andalucian, the bellows are from Marrakesh and the mirror and candlesticks are English.*

Detail of a fireplace decorated with antique tiles. Believed originally to have lined the ceiling of a palace in Seville or Cordoba, these tiles were found in the barn of a local farm. The mantelshelf is formed from Roman bricks and the dish is Portuguese.

This type of lantern with coloured glass panels was introduced by the Moors and is still made today. Here, a modern version lights the sitting room of a casita *with electricity, but formerly such lanterns would have held candles or oil lamps.*

FURNITURE

Furniture in Andalucian houses is unpretentious: wooden chairs usually have rush seats; small folding chairs and stools are based on designs introduced by the Moors and others. The *mesa camilla*, however, is exotic. It consists of a round table with built-in brazier for warmth on winter days.

A modern chair based on a traditional design with pine frame and rush seat, painted a dark, vibrant blue.

Washstands such as this, which is made of painted pine, were used before piped water was plumbed in. The elegant pot below is a type called a cantero, *used for cooling water.*

A mesa camilla. *No houses in Andalucia have heating other than the fireplace and stove, so the family would gather round a table like this in cold weather. Hot charcoal was laid in the centre of the lower tier. A heavy tablecloth had slits around the edge, which allowed the family to put their legs under the table to enjoy the heat.*

One corner of the sitting room on page 52 showing a small folding chair, a typical example of old Spanish furniture. The inspiration for it came from the days when Arab rulers travelled around the region, carrying their furniture with them. The little table is a traditional Spanish country piece.

One end of a long stool whose antique tooled leather top is formed from an old carriage seat.

An amuga, *a form of folding stool found in Ronda. The story goes that such stools were placed on horses' backs so that ladies could ride in relative comfort.*

A pine blanket chest with pretty iron lock, standing in front of a curtained window. The chest is a typical piece of Spanish furniture; the curtains are unusual for southern Spain and are made from fabric by the English designer George Spencer.

One of a pair of kitchen cupboard doors, the open lattice allowing air to circulate.

A mosaic of small tiles, some coloured green and blue and some plain terracotta, are laid in a tray to form a table top. The tiles are actually from north Africa, the Moorish influence clear to see.

KITCHENS

KITCHENS IN SOUTHERN SPAIN TEND TO BE
BRIGHT AND CHEERFUL, WITH A WELCOMING
ATMOSPHERE CREATED BY FLAMBOYANT,
COLOURFUL CERAMICS AND CHEQUERED
PATTERNS MADE FROM TILES OF MANY
COLOURS. PANS, BASKETS, DRIED HERBS AND
ASSORTED COOKING IMPLEMENTS HANG FROM
THE CEILINGS.

*Glass jars containing home-grown olives, typically
stored in brine rather than oil, and tomato sauce.*

Home-grown herbs and garlic hang from the ceiling of the kitchen of an English couple who have moved permanently to Andalucia and have converted and renovated a farm and surrounding buildings. The tiles and pots are all local.

These magnificent beams supporting the roof were once a ship's timbers. The pairs of doors were found in Ronda
and the pottery is all made locally in Andalucia. Herbs hanging from the ceiling include oregano, thyme and bay,
alongside a string of dried, home-grown red peppers.

The small green and white tiles which decorate the walls of this kitchen were hand made in Seville fifteen years ago. Similar tiles are often seen facing the outside of garden fountains in Andalucia.

China from Italy, Mexico and Spain in a white-painted plate rack. The bowl at the bottom is rough and unglazed on the outside, and is used to allow the dough to rise when making bread, or for standing milk in before skimming off the cream. The tiles are modern and made in Seville, with a star design based on Arabic decoration.

A recently painted old spice rack stores local Spanish pottery, Mexican painted gourds and, above, glass jars containing spices.

A busy kitchen is fitted with modern equipment but nonetheless has open lattice work on the cupboard doors –
the traditional way of allowing air to circulate.

BEDROOMS
&
BATHROOMS

BARE FLOORS AND SIMPLE IRON BEDSTEADS ARE

TYPICAL OF BEDROOMS, WHICH ARE ALMOST

INVARIABLY DECORATED IN AN UNFUSSY STYLE

WITH PLAIN PAINTED WALLS AND WOODEN

CEILINGS. BATHROOMS ARE COOL AND EQUALLY

UNPRETENTIOUS, WITH WHITE CHINA SET

AGAINST BRIGHTLY PATTERNED SPANISH TILES.

*A small mirror is framed by antique carriage lamps on
the wall of a cloakroom. The carved oak frame is one of
a pair and probably once contained a picture
rather than a mirror.*

A Spanish iron and brass bed is covered with a much-prized English patchwork quilt. The lamp stands in what was once the corner feeding trough for beasts stabled here, bearing witness to the house's agricultural origins.

Known as the 'blue bedroom', this was once a sheep shed. The window has been made recently and fitted with a frame of chestnut wood.

Hand-painted modern tiles from Seville provide a splashback in this cloakroom.
The antique mahogany corner cupboard was found by the owner in a junk shop.

Old brass taps on a modern basin in the bathroom (left). A curved corner unit has been created using tongue-and-groove planking in the doors. The pretty blue and yellow pot is typically Andalucian.

A modern bathroom in a cottage created out of an old stable. Plain white china looks dazzlingly fresh alongside blue-painted walls and modern blue-and-white locally made tiles.

ACKNOWLEDGEMENTS

DEDICATION

To my sister-in-law Helen

Elizabeth Hilliard would like to thank the many people whose kindness and enthusiasm have helped her with this book, but she is especially grateful to the following: Emma Armitage; Felicity Bryan and Michele Topham; Paul Burcher; Katrin Cargill; Wendy Dallas; Malcolm and Anne Davidson; Maria Foixa; Karen Hill; Alan James; Rachel King; Laurence Krzyzanek; Olivia Lowsley-Williams, who runs painting holidays at the Villa Santa Rosa in the province of Cadiz. For details phone or fax 34 5662 0052; Angus Mitchell, Tom Bell and Amparo Garrido, whose book, *Spain* (Weidenfeld & Nicolson) is such a delight; Diana Paget; Annabel Park; Charlotte Scott, who runs painting holidays at Trasierra in Cazalla de la Sierra. For details phone 34 5 488 43 24, or fax 34 5 488 33 05 (also for details of the chandelier on page 33); Helen Selka Farmiloe; William Selka; Maria José Sevilla; Elisabeth de Stroumillo; Nick Tudor; Rebecca Willis; Anna Wright.

Above all, she thanks John Miller whose beautiful photographs make this book what it is.